MW01243726

THE CHOICE OF UNFORGIVENESS

ROZ McNEIL

PRESS

TABLE OF CONTENTS

Introduction v
A Way of Life 7
Self-serving Pride or Humility? 10
What Controls You? 19
The Love of Forgiveness 21
My Desire for You 25
Those who Have Gone Before 27
The Blame Game 29
Transformed 32
To Be Like God 38
The Holy Spirit Will Lead You 43
How do Your Actions and Reactions
Measure up? 48
Forgive and Forget 52
Choose God's Love 57
The Source 66
Jonah's Dilemma 69
If You do not Forgive, You will not be Forgiven . .71
Memories 73
God's Loving Discipline 75
Conclusion 79

INTRODUCTION

I am writing this book because of what Father God has shown me through experiences I have been through and how I came to a place of forgiveness by seeing through His eyes and loving with His love. He has also taught me through what I have learned about experiences other people have been through. Most, if not all, people have been in a place of unforgiveness at least once in their lives.

By enduring and coming through to the other side with God, we learn that the act of forgiveness frees us to be all that God wants us to be. It strengthens us, nourishes us, and equips us.

Jesus said to them, "My food is to do the will of Him who sent Me and to accomplish His work." (John 4:34)

God is our sustenance when we do what He desires of us.

Forgiveness through obedience to God is like food: it is fulfilling; it gives us strength to do His will.

In the same way, unforgiveness brings bondage, starves us, and drains our strength because His will is not being done.

Be assured, you will not be able to forgive on your own, but God will help you. He will guide you, and He will lead you into the beautiful blessing of obedience.

The Lord is the one who goes ahead of you; He will be with you. He will not fail you or forsake you. Do not fear or be dismayed. **(Deuteronomy 31:8)**

The choice is yours!

I hope as you read this book, it will minister to your life in a positive way—a way that will bring glory to God through a renewed, restored, deeper relationship with Him, the intimacy that He truly desires to have with each one of us.

For those who do not yet have a relationship with the Father through Jesus Christ by the power of the Holy Spirit, I pray that this will draw you to Him, realizing your need for Him.

You will never be the same if you give yourself to this God of new beginnings!

He gives and He takes away. He will give you what is from Him and take away what is not from Him.

A Way Of Life

We begin this journey with an important fact: forgiveness should be a way of life. This does not mean that you always go back into the same situation or relationship you were in before forgiving someone. Trust may have to be earned again, but he or she will be able to freely choose how to react to your godlike behavior. You have done what God desires of you, and He will work with you and in you. You are pleasing God, and that is what matters. True obedience brings an intimacy with God that is beyond measure. I pray that you heed His command to forgive. It will bless you more than you can imagine.

God loves us so much that He wants us to be aware of how unforgiveness can attack the very fiber of our being. It can eat away at us until we are spiritually and sometimes physically changed in that it can cause all kinds of physical and mental problems as it takes control of us.

Have you ever done something that needed forgiving?

Have you ever wanted a second chance to prove yourself?

If you did not get that chance, how did it make you feel?

Do not allow unforgiveness to rule your life. The consequence of unforgiveness is that it affects you in a negative way. You are the one who suffers because of it, and it gives Satan a weapon to use against you, keeping you in bondage. Unforgiveness affects you physically as well as mentally because what we dwell on affects us positively or negatively.

It is said that letting go of grudges has surprising physical health benefits. Chronic anger (some think *constant* anger is a better word to use) is linked to decreased lung function, heart disease, stroke, and other ailments. Forgiveness will reduce anxiety, lower your blood pressure, and help you to breathe more easily. These benefits tend to increase as you get older (WedMD, January 21,2012).

Unforgiveness will eat at you until it affects every part of your life and the people in it. It will consume your thoughts, and you will even come to think of unforgiveness as a right that you have, and errantly you believe God understands.

God's Word continually reminds us of the importance of forgiveness, an action that He always displays.

Do you feel it is your right to hold on to unforgiveness?

Does this place of unforgiveness provide you comfort?

Has your physical or mental state been affected by your choice; for instance, never being truly happy?

SELF-SERVING PRIDE
OR HUMILITY?

I remember my mom having some problems with her siblings, and from time to time, they would show animosity towards one another. Sometimes it would get quite bad with little or no communication for a time. Sometimes things were said that caused only more hurt and anguish.

I was aware of problems in another family and shared with them the importance of forgiveness and of trying to make things right. I quoted this Scripture:

If possible, so far as it depends on you, be at peace with all men. **(Romans 12:8)**

The woman in this situation replied that she was not going to forgive and that God understood. She was so caught up in her feelings that she saw only what she felt. She was hurt, and maybe justifiably so, but pride entered in and was allowed to control her thoughts. She did not want to have anything to do with any of her family. Because of what happened to this woman, her husband held on to the same feelings.

We might look at this and say, "How can anyone think that!" I would like to think that a family like that is rare, but it is not. Sadly, I have seen other families harboring animosity toward one another in the same way.

I know of a family whose relationship with one another resulted in grievous hurt. When the mom died, she acknowledged one of her children with her wealth and disregarded the other two who had done much to help her and were always there for her. The one who received most of her money and possessions already had much and knowing the great need of one of the siblings chose to ignore it. The two who were left out still tried to reconnect with their sibling, but all communication was cut off. How utterly sad it is to see how people can treat one another!

Another incident comes to mind about two good friends who ended up at odds with each other all because of a misunderstanding. Something was said by one very innocently and received by the other as anything but. The offended one took what was said to heart and, instead of talking it over, stopped all communication with the first one. It was a sad time, as the first one could not understand the reason for the wedge that had come between them.

There was much anguish over the estrangement until one day, after a time, forgiveness was sought and given. What a waste of precious time before this came about! If only we would go to each other instead of letting the flesh take over. How much would be averted!

Is your family free from hurts, estrangements, harsh words, and jealousy that separate?

Have you wanted to try to close the rift with love, love that involves forgiveness?

Do you have a friend or friends with whom you have lost touch because of a misunderstanding?

Do you believe that God understands unforgiveness?

Families and relationships with others can be destroyed, whether the people involved are Christians or not, so this Scripture, although it is speaking to Christians, can definitely be used to show any family or relationship what can happen to them.

But if you are always biting and devouring one another, watch out! Beware of destroying one another. (Galatians 5:15 NLT)

It is so important to take the time to think and consider the consequences before you allow pride to enter in.

The act of attack can be so devastating that there may be nothing left to salvage.

Before we think, "How can people do this?" we must remember that it can happen to anyone who is not being led by the Holy Spirit.

***But I say, walk by the Spirit, and you will not carry out the desire of the flesh.* (Galatians 5:16)**

Christians especially, who know what God's Word says, still have to choose not to give in to the flesh. May I say to you that giving in to the flesh can be anything that we do that is the opposite of God's desire for us or anything we purpose to do under our own power.

Do you take time to think, pray, and get God's guidance before you say something to another?

Do you check your motives? Are they pure or self-serving?

Will your words heal or destroy?

Have you, as a Christian, ever had someone hurt you by what he or she said or did? It does not matter if it was intentional or not; it can happen. Have you forgiven that person or not forgiven that person?

You may have said to yourself, "I have forgiven," but realize that the offense still consumes too much of your thoughts and way too much of your time. Do you feel uneasy when you are around him or her?

Do you go out of your way to not be in the same place at the same time because even looking at this person brings back feelings that you have not dealt with?

Do you find it hard to pray for that man or woman?

Only by forgiving can you effectively pray for them.

Do you realize the precious time you are wasting by letting unforgiveness take up time that you could be spending doing the things that the Lord has for you to do, things that are beneficial for others as well as yourself.

A while back, our pastor brought up the fact that we all start the day with the same amount of time that God gives:86,400 seconds. We can choose to live our time—each second of each day—any way we want. How do you want to spend your 86,400 seconds: living in the freedom that God provides or in the prison that Satan provides? Satan's prison doors are always open as he tries to lure us in by whatever deception he can.

Have you ever said, "I have forgiven," but then did not want to be around him or her because you still felt uneasy?

Could it be that you really have not forgiven because, in your mind, the wounds are still too fresh?

Remember, *to hold back forgiveness* is not an entitlement for you. The thesaurus says that *entitlement* means "to have the right, prerogative, claim; permission, dispensation, privilege." We as God's children do not have the right to hold on to anything that He tells us to let go of.

Do you remember when you were forgiven of your sins and how it made you feel to know that you did not deserve forgiveness but received it because of God's great compassion and love for you exhibited in and through His Son on the cross?

Remember His love for you in that while we were yet sinners, Christ died for us. (Romans 5:8)

Forgiveness would not have been able to take place if Jesus had not taken our place. Oh, the all-consuming love He has for us!

God's Word says that we are to be like Him.

And become useful and helpful and kind to one another, tenderhearted (compassionate, understanding, loving-hearted), forgiving one another [readily and freely], as God in Christ forgave you. (Ephesians 4:32 AMP)

Therefore be imitators of God [copy Him and follow His example], as well-beloved children [imitate their father]. (Ephesians 5:1 AMP)

Do you feel God's love and compassion towards you as strongly now as you did when you first received His forgiveness?

If forgiveness came through a family member or a friend, how did that make you feel?

Unforgiveness is like someone whispering in your ear and saying to you, "Who do they think they are? You do not deserve to be treated this way." It causes a feeling of self-importance within you, continually adding fuel to the fire, anger burning within you.

Pride is the main cause of unforgiveness. Some Scriptures that address pride and humility are:

Pride goes before destruction, and a haughty spirit before stumbling. It is better to be humble in spirit with the lowly than to divide the spoil with the proud. (Proverbs 16:18-19)

But He gives a greater grace. Therefore it says, "God is opposed to the proud, but gives grace to the humble." ... Humble yourselves in the presence of the Lord, and He will exalt you. (James 4:6, 10)

For all that is in the world, the lust of the flesh and the lust of the eyes and the boastful pride of life, is not from the Father, but is from the world. (1 John 2:16)

16

These Scriptures are telling us that pride does not bless, honor, glorify, or please God. He is against pride and all that it stands for.

Micah speaks to what is essential in our walk with God:

> ***He has told you, O man, what is good; and what does the Lord require of you but to do justice, to love kindness, and to walk humbly with your God? (Micah 6:8)***

Forgiveness: pardon, absolution, exoneration, clemency, mercy; reprieve, amnesty; to pardon; to overlook an offense and treat the offender as not guilty. It is to show compassion and mercy.

Antonym: a word opposite in meaning to another (for example, *bad* and *good*).

So, unforgiveness would mean to be merciless and to punish; to hold on to the offense and the offender, treating him or her as guilty; to hold on to resentment; a desire to choose to punish. The only problem with that, again, is that holding unforgiveness can and will cause a wasting of self, through which ineffectiveness will prevail.

Therefore, forgiveness is healing to your body as well as your mind.

Unforgiveness works in the same way as forgiveness, although with opposite results. Whatever you choose to bring to mind is what you will dwell on; whatever you dwell on will live in your mind, grow, and eventually control your thoughts.

Unforgiveness, like weeds, will choke out the good, just like cultivating the good (forgiveness) will choke out the bad.

Did you realize that pride is the main factor in unforgiveness?

Did the anger preventing forgiveness ever take hold of you, telling you that you did not deserve to be treated or spoken to in such a way?

What do you dwell on?

WHAT CONTROLS YOU?

Do you want to be controlled by good thoughts or bad thoughts? What would be more beneficial to you? You are the one who will be affected the most.

If you let negative thoughts control you by playing over and over in your mind the bad thing or things that happened to you, it will become like a movie or, in this case, a bad movie that you know by heart because you have watched it so many times. You find some comfort in it, and therefore it has become a habit that you really do not want to turn off.

You probably have heard this before: 'Out with the bad and in with the good!' I pray that you embrace the fact that the only way to let the good in is to let the bad out.

Remember, God will help you. Do not allow a bad habit to rule you!

Let us take a little break here on our journey together on this road to forgiveness. We can think and talk about what a habit is and how it affects our lives. There is a park bench at the side of the road. We can sit there.

What kind of thoughts play in your mind: negative or positive?

Have you allowed a habit, good or bad, to control you?

Are you comfortable in this place you find yourself?

In many ways, habits are a big part of our lives, of who we are and how we live.

According to the dictionary, a *habit* is "a settled or regular tendency or practice, especially one that is hard to give up." This can develop into a bad habit.

The thesaurus says this about a habit: "custom, practice, routine, pattern, convention, way, norm, tradition, matter of course, rule, usage, etc. Habit of mind: disposition, temperament, character, nature, makeup, constitution, frame of mind, bent; accustomed to, used to, given to, inclined to."

Can you see how a habit could be bad or good, according to these definitions?

You can have a *habitude*, a habitual tendency or way of behaving.

I pray that our habitual tendencies will lead to what God desires of each of us who are His!

Okay, back on the road.

THE LOVE OF FORGIVENESS

To forgive is to love.

Above all things have intense and unfailing love for one another, for love covers a multitude of sins (forgives and disregards the offenses of others). **(1 Peter 4:8 AMP)**

F orgiveness is important for you to take hold of, whether it be for someone else or for yourself; unforgiveness will take hold of you in a detrimental (harmful) way.

Although the Bible does not speak of forgiving yourself, we must accept the forgiveness that God has for us and has provided for us. Otherwise, Satan will get a hold on us by bringing up our past, reminding us of how "bad" we are. He wants to get us into his vise. A vise is a metal tool with movable jaws that is used to hold an object firmly in place while work is done on it.

Satan will use guilt and unforgiveness as a vise to hold us in place while he works on us to bring us down. Do not let Satan bring you down by allowing the wrongs that you may have done in the past to keep you in the past. Remember, whatever we dwell on affects us for good or bad. *God forgives, and we need to walk in His forgiveness.*

God said that He forgives our sins when we repent and takes them from us. In the old covenant as well as in the new covenant, God forgives.

> ***Having canceled out the certificate of debt consisting of decrees against us, which was hostile to us; and He has taken it out of the way, having nailed it to the cross.* (Colossians 2:14)**

> ***Having cancelled and blotted out and wiped away the handwriting of the note (bond) with its legal decrees and demands which was in force and stood against us (hostile to us). This (note with its regulations, decrees, and demands) He set aside and cleared completely out of our way by nailing it to [His] cross.* (Colossians 2:14 AMP)**

> ***Having wiped out the handwriting of requirements that was against us, which was contrary to us. And He has taken it out of the way, having nailed it to the cross.* (Colossians 2:14 NKJV)**

I would like to take a close look at the Scripture that says:

As far as the east is from the west, so far has He removed our transgressions from us. (Psalm 103:12)

First, I would like to bring your attention to verse 10 which speaks volumes to us as a precursor to Psalm 103:12.

He [God] has not dealt with us according to our sins, nor rewarded us according to our iniquities [iniquities encompassing immoral or grossly unfair behavior]. (Psalm 103:10)

In other words, we do not get what we deserve. If we do not get what we deserve, how then can we withhold forgiveness from others?

Now, let us get off the road we are on for a while, sit under that tree, and talk about what "as far as the east is from the west" might mean.

To begin with, let us look at north and south. If you go north, you can keep going in a straight line until you reach the North Pole, and once you pass the North Pole, you begin going south. In essence, north runs into south and vice versa. Now if you start going east and keep walking in a straight line, you will always be going east, never west. The two do not meet at any point.

Longitude lines all meet at the poles, but latitude lines run parallel to each other.

Interesting, is it not? God puts your sins where they will never cross your path again! How exciting is that!

Oh, how He desires us to do as He does. I pray that the thought of how we felt when He forgave us will inspire us to want others to experience the same feeling.

What an indescribable love He has for us!

What do you think about love and forgiveness going hand in hand?

Has Satan ever reminded you of your past and the wrongs you have done, knowing that he wants to keep you there?

How did that make you feel, knowing God treats you as if you had never sinned?

Did you realize that you must receive God's forgiveness for yourself also?

MY DESIRE FOR YOU

efore we go on, I would like to present an opportunity for you.

My desire is to ask you to consider God. If you have not really given yourself to Him yet, you can do it right now. He will make all the difference in your life. He will become your life!

If you call out to God in faith, recognizing that you are a sinner and that you need Jesus, and repent of your sins, He will come in and change you. All He wants is a willing heart.

You can say something like this: "God, I realize that I am a sinner in need of a Savior. I believe that Jesus came, lived, suffered, died, and rose again for me. Only through His sacrifice could I become Your child. I repent of my sins and accept what Jesus did for me. I commit my life to You and receive eternal life from You. Thank You for a new beginning. I am now a new creation; the old is gone, and the new has come."

If you have prayed this prayer with a sincere heart, you are now a child of God; you have been 'Born Again.' You are just beginning your walk with Him, and what a walk it will be! I pray that you allow His Spirit to lead and direct you in all things. You are embarking on the most exciting time of your life.

Eternity with God starts now!

THOSE WHO HAVE GONE BEFORE

—◦◦◦—

F orgiveness for those who have already gone is essential to a healthy mind and body as well.

For whatever reason you have not forgiven someone, you need to do it now, whether or not the person or people are alive. Let it go. Life is too precious to dwell on whatever happened in the past. Instead, use the past to learn from and to grow from and to help others who may be going through some of the same circumstances. God will get the glory, and you will be blessed above and beyond what you can imagine.

If you still feel that you will not forgive, think about it. Is it because you feel comfortable in the place of unforgiveness? Is it like giving something up, but in reality not really wanting to give it up, so you keep going back to retrieve it and bring it "home" with you? You would be hanging on to something that will never give you true peace. I implore you not to allow yourself to entertain a "guest" that will destroy you.

Have you ever thought that you wished you had forgiven someone, but then it was too late?

Do you realize that it is never too late because forgiveness, like unforgiveness, comes from the heart, and it is an action that you take that releases you and sets you free from the past?

THE BLAME GAME

Unforgiveness shows itself in many ways. One such way is the blame game.

Everything you have done, have chosen to do, you blame on others. For instance, you may say, "My parents treated me such and such a way, so it is their fault I did this or that!" This may be true and may not be true. It may only be from your perspective. Many times when looking back, you realize it was not exactly how you envisioned it. I went that route at one time.

As I was growing up, I felt that I was not as close to my parents as I wanted to be. Whether it was true or not, that is the way I felt. I grew to have a low opinion of myself. I wanted the love I felt was missing from my life, so I did various things to try to attain it. I was always trying to prove myself.

By the way, low self-esteem can be as prideful as one who is lofty; because we are focusing on ourselves, we feed off it. By feeling sorry for ourselves, maybe thinking we are worthless, we want others to continually lift us up to make us feel better. After all, it is only because we "never had a chance," right? Well, I thought that before I came to know my Lord.

I bought into the lie that Satan told me, reminding me of how unworthy and how bad I really was and that I did not deserve anything better. Every time I did something wrong, I would blame my parents. It was their fault, not mine! I became rebellious.

I did not have a relationship with God at the time, but I knew enough to talk to Him, or rather, bargain with Him, whenever I got into trouble. Repeatedly I would remind Him that it was not my fault—it was because of my parents. *Oh, how easy it is to play the blame game!*

One day He showed me, as only He can, that I was old enough to take responsibility for my own actions and that I had nobody else to blame but myself. Well, that was some revelation to me!

Ever since God revealed that truth to me, I have never forgotten it. It pertains to me and to everyone else who will not take responsibility for what they choose to do.

Do you see that if you are not taking responsibility for your actions or lack of actions, you still have only yourself to blame? Even when you decide to do nothing, you are still making a choice.

What is so wonderful about God is that He will break through even when we do not know Him. He did this with me, convicting me with His truth. Even then, a time when I was still separated from

Him and on my way to hell, He lovingly spoke to my heart. He cares so deeply for each one of us, giving us every chance to come to Him. I still did not have a relationship with Him, but I remembered the revelation I received.

Have you ever blamed anyone else for what you chose to do?

Have you ever felt that you were the victim?

Has the revelation that you are responsible for your own actions ever come to your mind?

TRANSFORMED

There came a time when all of my self-degrading thoughts and actions came to a halt. I came to the place of being aware that the feeling of never being satisfied could be satisfied only with God.

I came to realize that it was not what I was searching for that would fulfill me. It was who, although I was unaware until the need for Jesus became as apparent as my need for the next breath I would take! When I cried out to Him, I received the love, forgiveness, the acceptance, the everything I was looking for.

What Satan meant for destruction, God used for salvation. I was keenly aware of how unworthy I was and so undeserving, but these facts finally brought me to Him. In ourselves, we are unworthy, undeserving, but *God's love covers all*, and we become His with all that entails. He took our place so that we could choose to take our place with Him. Oh, what love He has for you and me—a love that envelops us with His presence!

When I became a child of God, one of the first things I did was to ask my parents and some others to forgive me for whatever I had done to hurt them. I knew with all my heart that as my Father God had forgiven me, I needed not only to forgive others, but also to ask for forgiveness as well. I could hardly wait to talk to my dad and mom. I loved them and wanted so much for them and everyone to experience God in the way that He desires us to know Him.

I had a revelation of what it really meant to experience God's love–the love I had been searching for! I wanted to show that love to others so they could know the joy of being His; a joy words cannot express. I did not want to allow anything to keep me in bondage to the "old life."

I desperately wanted the whole world to feel and know God's love for themselves. I started sharing with anyone I could the joy that I felt as the result of being His.

In the beginning God created the heavens and the earth. (Genesis 1:1)

God the Father created the heavens and the earth and all that it contains through the Son in the power of the Spirit. The God who spoke things into existence I could now call my Father!

My Father God was the one who would always love me (unconditionally) and hold me and pick me up if I fell. Jesus went to the cross (the execution stake) and took all that was due me upon

Himself to give me the chance to become His. Now I had the Father and the Son living in my spirit through His Holy Spirit! I was filled with the excitement of a little child.

If you have become a child of God, what was the turning point in your life that caused you to run to Him?

Were you aware of your desperate need that only He could satisfy?

How did you feel when you experienced His all-encompassing love for you?

When my earthly dad died, I wanted to speak at his memorial. Thoughts of the past kept coming into my mind that reminded me of the things that I had not done with my dad and of what my sister had done with our dad.

It surprised me as I wondered why I would think of negative things from the past. I found myself somewhat jealous of my sister and of what she had with our dad and mom.

I could not think of things to say about my relationship with my dad at his funeral. I seemed to have a block. I could, however, say a lot about my sister and her relationship with our dad.

The Holy Spirit showed me something one day as I was thinking of all that my dad and I did not have in common and how I had always wanted to be closer to him.

I saw a dark cloud mushrooming right before my eyes. It was the way I was seeing things in my mind. The cloud blocked everything else out. He said that I was dwelling on the negative so much that I could not see anything else and only when I chose to let the negative go would I see the positive.

Do any past feelings try to block your vision?

Do you ever dwell on the negative in your past that you thought was taken care of?

Does your past jealousy ever try to rear its ugly head?

Therefore if anyone is in Christ, he is a new creature; the old things passed away; behold, new things have come. (2 Corinthians 5:17)

Therefore if any person is [ingrafted] in Christ (the Messiah) he is a new creation (a new creature altogether); the old [previous moral and spiritual condition] has passed away. Behold, the fresh and new has come. (2 Corinthians 5:17 AMP)

Fresh and new. Wow, think of what that means! The past, my old life without God, is no longer; now everything I need or desire is in Christ.

Can you imagine what that meant to me? That truth does not wane but gets stronger the more you draw to Him. Through my transformation, I was able to see things through God's eyes. What a beautiful view seen through His eyes! I could now see around and through that mushroom cloud that blocked my view. You can too if you put your trust in the One who is able and willing to help you.

I am not saying it always happens right away. Some things might take a while, but putting into practice what God is telling you will cause the right outcome. When you choose forgiveness, it may take a short time or a long time to allow it to permeate your thinking, but you must make the decision to forgive and not wait any longer. Remember, with God anything is possible.

> *Now to Him who is able to do far more abundantly beyond all that we ask or think, according to the power that works within us, to Him be the glory in the church and in* **Christ Jesus to all generations forever and ever. Amen. (Ephesians 3:20-21)**

We now have help to do the will of God through the grace of God in and through the power of His Spirit. When we recognize that we can do nothing without God's help and rely on Him and His strength, we allow Him to work through our weaknesses, showing Himself strong. We unite with Him to accomplish His desires in our life as we draw from Him. *If we give our all to Him, we can draw all from Him. There is no greater joy than being His.*

I am a child of the King! I now belong happily, fully, completely to Him!

And though you have not seen Him, you love Him, and though you do not see Him now, but believe in Him, you greatly rejoice with joy inexpressible and full of glory. **(1 Peter 1:8)**

I was filled with joy unspeakable (inexpressible) and full of glory!

Full of glory; full: containing or holding as much as possible; having no empty space; completely engrossed with; unable to stop talking or thinking about; not lacking or omitting anything; complete.

Here is an even deeper understanding:

Without having seen Him, you love Him; though you do not [even] now see Him, you believe in Him and exult and thrill with inexpressible and glorious (triumphant, heavenly) joy. [At the same time] you receive the result (outcome, consummation) of your faith, the salvation of your souls. **(1 Peter 1:8 AMP)**

Have you thought about being a new creation? How does that make you feel?

Do you realize what seeing through the eyes of the Father is like? Is there any more beautiful view?

Do you feel the importance of acting as He does?

Does the desire to forgive in obedience to Him now lead you to do it?

To Be Like God

⟡⟡⟡

You may have said to yourself many times that you want to be like God, following His example. If we are to be obedient to God and be like Him, we must think about how He treats us.

Jesus, God the Son, came to earth as a man to take our place, to pay the penalty due us. He bought and paid for us with His blood, His sacrifice. He took our place on that execution stake. He did for us what we could not do for ourselves. He opened the way for us to become children of God by taking our sins upon Himself.

> *And Jesus cried out again with a loud voice, and yielded up His spirit. And behold, the veil of the temple was torn in two from top to bottom; and the earth shook and the rocks were split.* **(Matthew 27:50–51)**

The veil represented the holiness of the temple that the priests went into with much trepidation. If they did wrong, they might not come out alive.

Now the way to the Father was open to all who would come. Now we could have a relationship with God that no works of our own could accomplish. Jesus already accomplished what we could not. We who become His no longer need someone else to act in our stead; we can go directly to Him. Now we are called priests.

But you are a chosen race, a royal priesthood, a dedicated nation, [God's] own purchased, special people that you may set forth the wonderful deeds and display the virtues and perfections of Him Who called you out of darkness into His marvelous light. **(1 Peter 2:9 AMP)**

This is what you, we, become a part of when we become His.

Do you see that the darkness you were in before you chose to accept Jesus and what He did for you, and His light, which you now inhabit and are inhabited by, are total opposites? This Light who delivered us out of something dark, sinful, and negative has brought us into a holy place—His place—a shelter, a refuge, the place He desires us to abide. We are to be holy temples for His Holy Spirit to dwell in.

We are to be like Him! We are to imitate Him!

Again, we are to act and react as He does.

Be kind to one another, tenderhearted, forgiving each other, just as God in Christ also has forgiven you. (Ephesians 4:32)

You are to forgive just as God in Christ also has forgiven you.

How does it feel to be counted as part of a chosen race, a royal priesthood?

How does it make you feel knowing that your past sins that separated you from God have been forgiven and you can now enter into His very presence?

How does it make you feel to know that you were delivered out of darkness and that you are now filled with His light?

Forgive just as He has forgiven you. What if you had not been forgiven? The truth be known, none of us deserved to be forgiven. Would you agree? How did you feel when you received His forgiveness?

Do you grasp the fact that Jesus paid the price, which is condemnation, for you and me because of His love for us and because He is the only one who could. Can you imagine what kind of love that takes? In our own selves, we cannot come close to comprehending the depth of the love God has for us.

But God demonstrates His own love toward us, in that while we were yet sinners, Christ died for us. (Romans 5:8)

Luke tells us about the prodigal son in **(Luke 15:11-32 paraphrase)**: The young man thought only of himself and what pleased him as he took his inheritance and squandered it. In essence, he had to do a very menial job feeding pigs and was so destitute that he would have gladly eaten the food the pigs ate. He came to his senses and realized that he wanted to go home and ask his father if he could be treated as one of his servants because he was not worthy to be called his son.

While he was on his way, his father saw him from a distance and ran to meet him. His father had compassion on him, embraced him, and kissed him. He asked his servants to bring his son the best robe, a ring for his hand, and shoes for his feet, and to kill the fatted calf and have a party to welcome him home. The father was full of love and forgiveness for his son.

That is how our Father God wants us to act. He is our example. How can we who have received God's full forgiveness keep it from someone else?

The problem in this story was with the older brother. He acted a lot like we do in the flesh. He was not forgiving and was angered that his father would do such a thing. The older brother kept recalling what the younger brother had done and refused to go in to the party. His father came out to entreat him to come in, but all he could think of was that his younger brother had not gotten what he deserved, and he did not want to forgive him. He chose unforgiveness.

Do not be as the older brother, but be as the father who welcomed the repentant son with open arms and forgiveness.

Remember, God welcomes us with open arms.

Try to imagine yourself as the prodigal son and as the older brother who displayed unforgiveness. Can you feel the emotions the older brother was going through? Do you see how unhealthy that is—how his reactions fed his actions?

We were unworthy, undeserving, and in sin. Christ covered us with His love!

For Christ did not enter a holy place made with hands, a mere copy of the true one, but into heaven itself, now to appear in the presence of God for us; nor was it that He would offer Himself often, as the high priest enters the holy place year by year with blood that is not his own. Otherwise, He would have needed to suffer often since the foundation of the world; but now once at the consummation of the ages He has been manifested to put away sin by the sacrifice of Himself. (Hebrews 9:24–26)

Have you ever found yourself in the wrong place because of your choices and wanted to go back to where you belong?

Have you ever found yourself in the place of the jealous brother who held unforgiveness in his heart?

The Holy Spirit Will Lead You

———〜〜〜———

**But I say, walk by the Spirit, and you
will not carry out the desire of the flesh.
(Galatians 5:16)**

I f you do not allow the Holy Spirit to lead you,
the devil will be more than happy to lead you
down the path of destruction.

Has something ever happened to you that
hurt you in a deep way? Have you found it easy
to forgive, or have you held resentment?

Consider this: Your spouse has hurt your feelings in anger or in other ways, intentionally or
unintentionally. Instead of forgiving him or her,
you feel as though you want someone, anyone,
to know how you have been hurt. You reason
in your mind that if you tell someone, he or she
can pray with you for your situation, when all
you really want is someone else to feel sorry
for you or to be as angry as you are about how
your spouse has been treating you. It becomes

nothing other than a form of retribution. You want to hurt him or her like you were hurt.

Do not let it be all about you. The devil is into division, not reconciliation. He wants to cause havoc in your marriage; he wants you to fail. Please pray to God and get His counsel before you do anything. You will be blessed and will be a blessing in return. It may seem hard at first, but press in. You will be rewarded with a closer walk with God.

If you do not forgive, the evil one will make sure to bring the offenses up to you increasingly until you are consumed with negative thoughts about your loved one or anyone else you have a problem with.

It may not be intentional, in your mind, to hold on to negative feelings, but they will definitely be a result of your choosing unforgiveness. Your thoughts will take you to a place you do not want to be.

Remember, unforgiveness affects you more than the one you do not forgive. It will come to mind at the most inopportune times. You will be doing something and it will invade your mind, and you will start thinking about the one or ones who made you sad, mad, indignant.

Your thoughts will affect your actions. You might say, "They do not deserve forgiveness after what they have done," or "I am not the one who needs to forgive," or "God is the one who forgives; it is not up to me." In reality, it is up to you to forgive!

Peter had a question for the Lord Jesus as recorded in Matthew about forgiveness:

Then Peter came and said to Him, "Lord, how often shall my brother sin against me and I forgive him? Up to seven times?" Jesus said to him, "I do not say to you, up to seven times, but up to seventy times seven." **(Matthew 18:21-22)**

Jesus wanted Peter to know that we must forgive every time someone asks for forgiveness; the purpose of 490 times was to show that no one is likely to keep track of every time he forgives someone. God's intention is that forgiveness becomes so much a part of our lives that it will become automatic.

Jesus' response to Peter came by way of a parable about a king. The essence of the passage is this: A king wished to settle accounts with his slaves. One slave owed him much money and could not pay. The slave asked the king for patience until he could repay what he owed. The king felt compassion for the slave and forgave him the debt.

You would have thought the slave, receiving forgiveness, would act in kind, but he did the opposite. The forgiven slave went out and found one of his fellow slaves who owed him money, attacked him, and demanded the money. When his fellow slave pleaded with him for patience until he could repay, he refused and had him thrown into prison until he could pay back what was owed. This was reported to the king, who was very angry because the first slave did not show the same compassion and mercy that was shown him, and he punished him for his actions.

The point is this: The first slave could do nothing to repay what was owed and relied on the mercy and compassion of the king. He was forgiven his debt, just as we are forgiven our debt when we come to the King. It has nothing to do with our earning it or meriting it. **(Read the parable in Matthew 18:23-35)**

We who receive love and forgiveness from God do not have the right to withhold forgiveness from another. If we choose unforgiveness, we lose our right standing with the One who forgives and forgets. We will be held accountable for our actions, and unforgiveness is definitely an action that draws the one who makes this choice away from all that is important.

We are to do as God does with us. God has revealed to me that whether someone asks for forgiveness or not, we are still to forgive them. Whether they are aware of what they have done or not, our action is forgiveness. If what someone else does to us in thought, word, or deed affects us in a negative way, we are to forgive them. It will benefit us immensely as we see them through the eyes of God!

Have you ever said that it was not up to you to forgive, but that God is the one who forgives?

Have you ever shared with someone that you had been hurt only because you wanted them to feel the anger you felt about the one who hurt you?

How do you feel about the fact that God is asking you to forgive even if forgiveness was not asked for?

Do you believe that forgiveness can become in you a way of living, that it can be automatic?

Do you desire to be obedient to God's will?

How Do Your Actions And Reactions Measure Up?

⚬⚬⚬

Have you ever shaken your fist or said an unholy word or words when someone in another vehicle cut you off or did something else to offend or anger you? Try forgiving him or her, and ask God to bless them and protect them. Pray that if the driver does not have a personal relationship with God, that God will send someone into his or her life that very day who will witness to the fact that Jesus loves them. *By your actions, you may be that very one!*

You might say, "What a novel idea"—with an amused look on your face—"if I could just get past the shaking of my fist at the offender or stop the offensive word or words from coming out of my mouth long enough to forgive and pray for him or her."

Trust me, or rather, trust God, if you allow the Holy Spirit to work through you, in obedience to Him and with help from Him, you will be able to do it. This is the very thing that He put on my heart to do when I started getting angry with some drivers.

I realized, as I tried putting myself in their shoes, that I also had made unintentional mistakes at times and hoped that others would forgive me.

Even if the driver intentionally cut me off or did not let me out or whatever, I was told to forgive. The circumstances really did not matter. In obedience, I started to do that very thing and came to feel God's love toward "whomever."

This was just one case, but I was reminded again, as I had been reminded so many times before, that everyone is important to Him, and they should be to us. After all, we are to be like Him.

Therefore, be imitators of God, as dearly loved children. And walk in love, as the Messiah also loved us and gave Himself for us, a sacrificial and fragrant offering to God. (Ephesians 5:1-2 HCSB)

We can use each opportunity we find ourselves in to curse or to bless. Why not bless instead? Believe me, it will become a habit the more you do it, and you will feel much better for it. It is God's way, and doing things God's way will bring you many blessings.

I know someone who came from a large family. There came a time when any harmony or love within the family, save a small amount, was no longer. There was much disharmony, quarreling, and mistrust. The most devastating outcome was unforgiveness.

They would not see any side but their side. Feelings were hurt. Words that were spoken cut like knives. Wounds that were caused by words and actions festered, and the balm that would have healed the wounds was not used. Division seemed to be the rule—not at all as God had intended. Any closeness or affection for one another seemed to be gone.

One of the family told me that she would not forgive and that God understood. May I tell you that God does not understand! He is all about forgiveness. That family member chose unforgiveness and believed that it was okay with God! Obviously, the result of the actions most of the family took did not bring restoration, but only discord.

Oh, how important words are! Words can heal, and words can destroy. We can do so much damage with our words, and we can do so much good with our words. The tongue can set a fire ablaze or be the instrument used to put a fire out.

By our words, we can encourage or discourage, build up or tear down.

Most of you have heard the saying:"Sticks and stones can break your bones, but words will never hurt you." Many will tell you that the opposite is true. Words can do much more damage than any physical action.

It only takes one person to undo a wrong, at least where he or she is concerned, according to his or her ability.

***If possible, so far as it depends on you, be at peace with all men.* (Romans 12:18)**

***Depart from evil and do good; seek peace and pursue it.* (Psalm 34:14)**

God is interested in the actions you take, no matter what others do. Are you treating others as He intends or as you decide? Are you drawing from your experiences, or are you letting go of them and going on with God?

Unforgiveness will blind you to the truth. You will not be able to see past that cloud of negativity that you have placed before you. All you will focus on is yourself and how you were hurt, how you were treated. You will say, "How dare they!" or "How could they!"

Have you ever gotten angry with a driver who got in your way or who cut you off or slowed you down?

Have you ever been angry with someone who got in front of you as you were about to enter the checkout lane at a store or who pulled in to a parking spot just as you were about to?

Have you ever spoken harsh words to someone in anger and wished you could take those words back?

FORGIVE AND FORGET

E ven if you or someone you know does not remember the wrong done, you or they do remember the one who did it or caused it, and that fact keeps it alive in your mind. In the same way, if you let God work in you, you can choose to let the people go by forgiving them and therefore not bring the offense to mind.

The more you concentrate on forgiving, the more you forget what was done. This choice will free you; it will free you from bondage to do the things that God desires of you.

Remember, if you think that you can start forgiving and forgetting on your own, it will not work. *Only with God are positive decisions possible. He will work through your weaknesses and cause you to be strong because He will be at work in you.*

If you still decide to hang on to unforgiveness, remember that harboring unforgiveness will allow it to attach itself to you like a cancer. It will loom over you like an ominous dark cloud. It will steal your joy. It will affect your life in a negative way.

You will find excuses and reasons to justify your choice. You might say to yourself, "I can forgive, but I cannot forget." You have already decided that you cannot or will not forget. May I say to you that you are not forgiving if you will not forget! I say, "Will not" because you alone make the decision, and you alone can choose to dwell on the offense or let it go.

Do you ever say that you can forgive, but not forget?

Have you allowed unforgiveness to attach itself to you by

justifying your choice? And it is your choice!

God forgets as well! Can you imagine Him saying, "I have forgiven, but I can never forget?" No, He would never say that. He does not remind you of your past sins. He does not want your past to hold you, and that is what would happen.

God not only forgives us our sins, but He also does not bring them to mind again.

If *you choose not to forget*, it opens the way for Satan to torment you with pictures and words in your mind that will continually remind you, to validate in your mind that you are right in your choice. If you do not choose to forget with God's help, you will not forgive because you will harbor constant reminders, and by doing this, you will not be acting as God does.

I, even I, am the one who wipes out your transgressions for My own sake,

and I will not remember your sins.
(Isaiah 43:25)

***For I will be merciful to their iniquities,
and I will remember their sins no more.***
(Hebrews 8:12)

*Again, this statement, "I will remember their
sins no more," does not mean that God cannot
remember our sins, but that He chooses not to—
as if they had never happened.*

Now that is love!

We can choose, with the help of the Holy
Spirit, not to bring offenses to mind again. If we
practice putting the wrongs done to us out of
our minds, we will eventually see that person or
people as God sees them—through His eyes.

There is no better way than to see as God
sees. Yes, Satan will try to keep the offense
before you saying, remember when he or she
said this or did that, remember how they made
you feel, remember the hurt it caused you;
remember, remember, remember!

You may pull over to the side of the road
because you are driving and your eyes are filled
with tears, so much so that it is hard to see. Then
you are reminded by God that you need to forgive. You must forgive; it is the only way that you
can have peace, the peace that comes only from
obeying God. So you say to Satan that you have
forgiven and you will continue to forgive because
that is the way of Father God.

Jesus gave all so that you could receive all that He has for you. Do not allow Satan to steal that from you.

"*The thief [is the one who] comes only to steal, and to kill, and to destroy.*" (John 10:10)

Satan will try to steal your joy, kill you or your faith, and destroy your testimony. Do not give him the power to do this.

The good news is in remembering the rest of the Scripture, when Jesus goes on to say, **"*I came that they may have life, and have it abundantly.*"**

Jesus gives life! Satan brings death.

Do you remember that the Holy Spirit will help you practice forgiveness until it becomes a habit?

Who wants to keep those offenses fresh in your mind?

Our strength comes from our joy, and our joy comes from the Lord. This is the strength that *we need* to overcome!

Do not be grieved, for the joy of the Lord is your strength. (Nehemiah 8:10)

For we walk by faith, not by sight. (2 Corinthians 5:7)

Faith (complete trust or confidence; belief) is in God. We are to live by faith. Faith believes and then receives.

***Now faith is the assurance of things hoped for, the conviction of things not seen.* (Hebrews 11:1)**

We live to and for God.

***No weapon formed against you will prosper.* (Isaiah 54:17)**

You are the one who needs to come against the schemes of Satan by standing and pro-claiming God's Word. Remember, you have the power and the authority in Jesus' name. Believe it, and use it!

Everything we need is in God.

Do you take time to read what God's Word says to you?

Do you know that His Word is life?

What do you think about standing on God's Word, His truth,

regardless of what is going on around you?

CHOOSE GOD'S LOVE

I got a surprise the other day. It was unexpected, but it showed me how quickly the flesh can try to take over.

I found myself feeling agitated and a little angry at something two people said. What was said bothered me as it was about me. I found myself wanting to defend myself even though it was not something worth defending. The more I thought about it, the more irritated I became. God reminded me that it was not important and that I needed to let it go. He also reminded me that this feeling was a type of unforgiveness.

I was hanging on to the agitation. This is how wrong thoughts or harboring wrong thoughts can affect you. It takes over and your focus is back on you, right where it should not be. These thoughts can creep up when you least expect them to. I forgave and thought that maybe what was said was misunderstood in the way it was said. I let it go.

Sometimes people do not realize that they have offended you; it is just the way you perceived it and received it.

Again, it is your place to forgive. You need to forgive, and the sooner the better, or else something of little importance will turn into something of big importance; and it can happen very easily.

Satan and self feed on delay. How we react, he reacts. If we are slow to act in doing the right thing, he will try to make *slow* become *never.* This is why we need to practice forgiveness, to come to that place where it is an automatic response.

If something you heard still bothers you, it is better to talk to the people and work it out. It is never worth holding on to anger. This talk turns into an opportunity to practice forgiveness. Whoever is in the wrong or in the right does not matter. What matters is to address your feelings right away and forgive, whether you have to tell the person or just acknowledge it to yourself.

God showed me a truth one time that started me thinking about writing this book. I was thinking about a situation in which I found that I was holding on to wrong feelings and that, in actuality, I was harboring unforgiveness. God said to me that I needed to forgive. I replied, "No one asked me to forgive." He then said that I should not wait until someone asked me; I needed to automatically forgive and forgive now. I then replied that I wanted to be obedient to Him, but I wanted to make sure I was ready. I told Him that I did not want to say, "I forgive" and then not really forgive.

When I was ready, I would be happy to oblige! He then told me that if I waited until I was ready, it would never happen.

I entered into a time of blaming myself for things that I had done wrong that helped cause this mess. I kept hearing in my head, "If you had done this instead of that, it would not have happened." Do you remember when you acted that way, remember when you did that, remember when you said that; 'it is your fault.'

These thoughts would come to me when I least expected them, and then they would come a lot. This all occurred after I started forgiving.

Satan was trying to pull me down, make me focus on myself, and make me get in and stay in a depressed mood. Yes, Satan will attack you in a moment by reminding you that it is or was your fault and then continually bring it to your mind so that you will be so obsessed with "fault" that you cannot seem to get past it. *Do not let that happen!*

See yourself as one who has received God's forgiveness. Walk and live as one who is forgiven. In so doing, Satan will have no recourse, no place to go with his accusations.

If we choose to be at odds with God by being disobedient, out of His will, we cannot be used as He desires in carrying out His plan for us.

It is important to be honest with God and with yourself. Remember, your relationship with God the Father, the Son, and the Holy Spirit is what life is all about. Do not allow Satan or yourself to make it all about you. God alone is always the only one we should focus on.

Have you ever taken to heart what someone said to you or what someone said about you?

Have you ever thought that maybe what was said was misunderstood by you and not meant the way it sounded?

Were you angry about what was said?

Did you let go of the anger and forgive?

When Scripture says to bless those who curse, persecute, and despitefully use you, it speaks to what blesses our Father God. Here are four Scriptures that speak to commandments from God about how we are to react to personal attacks:

But I say to you, love your enemies and pray for those who persecute you. (Matthew 5:44)

Bless those who curse you, pray for those who mistreat you. (Luke 6:28)

Bless those who persecute you; bless and do not curse. (Romans 12:14)

And we toil, working with our own hands; when we are reviled, we bless, when we are persecuted, we endure. (1 Corinthians 4:12)

It is easy to love and bless and pray for those who love you and who treat you well and speak well of you, but to love, bless, pray for, and speak softly or speak a good word to one who has harshly accused you, to love those who do not love in return or who may even hate you, to speak well of them and not gossip about them, is harder to accomplish. *Realizing the truth that only through God can we do anything that is good, that is required of us, we surrender our flesh to His will, and in doing so, we are most blessed of all.*

Asking God to bless those who persecute me or hurt me in thought, word, or deed does not mean that I am asking Him to bless them because of what they chose to do, but rather, to bless them by having other Christians come alongside to tell them about God and His love. I pray for more opportunities for them to know Him through conviction and in knowing that He does not hold on to what they have done in the past or hold a grudge against them or unforgiveness; what God does is exhibit love, forgiveness and a new beginning, a new life—a life that is filled with a joy that transcends all other joy if they choose to become His.

I believe God desires it to become common-place for us to automatically react in the way that is pleasing to Him. I ask you to take this thought captive: How could you bless in a more profound way one who has hurt, persecuted, or cursed you in thought, word, or deed than to *forgive* him or her, emulating God who dwells in you.

I love the word *emulate*. It means "to imitate; reproduce the function or action of; to mirror, follow, model oneself on." One place I feel the apostle Paul eloquently speaks to this is in this Scripture:

> ***Therefore be imitators of God as dear children. And walk in love, as Christ also has loved us and given Himself for us, an offering and a sacrifice to God for a sweet-smelling aroma.* (Ephesians 5:1-2 NKJV)**

The author C. S. Lewis was quoted as saying, "To be a Christian means to forgive the inexcusable because God has forgiven the inexcusable in you." This quote is from his "Essay on Forgiveness." So if you are a Christian, apparently you have no excuse to not forgive.

Let us take a step backwards into the present. If God had not forgiven you your sins when you chose to become His, where would you be right now? Think about it. Take your time. Does this change your perspective? Can you still say, "It is not up to me to forgive because God is the one who forgives?" That is not only a lie, but also the response that Satan would have you think. Remember, we are to act and react as our Father God does.

I pray that we would all step back and look into our present to see where we might be if we were unforgiven. May I tell you, we would be in the worst place imaginable!

Remember His Word telling *us* to forgive also. Here are some Scriptures that are undeniable:

***And forgive us our debts, as we also have forgiven our debtors.* (Matthew 6:12)**

***For this is My blood of the covenant, which is poured out for many for forgiveness of sins.* (Matthew 26:28)**

***This is My commandment, that you love one another, just as I have loved you.* (John 15:12)**

***This means that anyone who belongs to Christ has become a new person. The old life is gone; a new life has begun!* (2 Corinthians 5:17 NLT)**

***He has rescued us from the domain of darkness and transferred us into the kingdom of the Son He loves. We have redemption, the forgiveness of sins, in Him.* (Colossians 1:13–14 HCSB)**

Can you see how these Scriptures relate to our forgiveness and to our forgiving others?

If we hold unforgiveness, it means that we are not loving one another as He loves us, so in essence, we are not really loving God as we should.

Love is an action as well as a reaction. Real love does not hold on to a wrong done but embraces the one who committed the wrong with forgiveness. It does not deny the sin or pretend it did not happen, but it calls sin by its name and does not withhold forgiveness from the one who repents.

If we focus on the wrong done to us, whether real or imagined, whether intentional or unintentional, we will not be able to see beyond that or get beyond that. We will again be stuck in the muck and the mire that God delivered us from; we will be bound to our choice of unforgiveness.

I ask you to ponder this, as I have seen it happen so many times: families in which parents have not forgiven their children for some hurt they have caused them and children not forgiving their parents for the same reason. I urge you, if you are in this situation, no matter what the cause of the problem, do not hold on to unforgiveness. If something happens to your children or your parents, you will have a hard time getting over the fact that you had a chance to make things right and did not take it. Go to them, if you are able, and talk to them. You will be blessed by being instrumental in working it out.

There are parents who have treated their children differently. One may be held in a higher regard than the other; one may be loved more than the other. Although children are different, they still desire and need the same love. Anger, resentment, and animosity can rise up in the family and lead to a place of almost no return.

Let me inject here that God would not, does not, and never will treat one of His children in a different way from another. He treats each of us as if we were His only child. His love for us is everlasting, unconditional, and unchanging.

For He Himself has said, "I will never desert you, nor will I ever forsake you." (Hebrews 13:5)

We become one with Him. Oh, how glorious!
Because of choices we have made in the past or even after we become His, we may feel unworthy of God's love, but remember, *we are only worthy because of what Jesus did for us.*

Have you ever held resentment, anger, or animosity against a member of your family?

Have you ever hated the sin but loved the sinner with the love of God?

Have you ever imagined where you would be now if not for the forgiveness of God?

THE SOURCE

I am reminded of David in 1 Samuel 30:6. David was greatly distressed because the people spoke of stoning him, for all the people were embittered, each one because of his sons and his daughters. David was distressed, probably thinking of all that had happened and that he was to blame. I can almost hear him saying to God, "I know You are with me in spite of everything I am and everything I am not." He was told what the people were saying about him, all the things that were negative about him, but he knew that he could call on his Lord for strength, hope, and help.

He went to the source, the One who he knew would always be there for him no matter what, the only one who could meet his need. David needed to hear what God, not man, said about him.

The devil is always ready to point out what is or was wrong with us. God does not see us in that way.

"David strengthened himself in the Lord his God." **(1 Samuel 30:6)**

He was emboldened by going to God.

As God emboldened David, so He will do for you if you go to Him. His very Word encourages and strengthens you by reading it with the aid of His Spirit and taking His promises to yourself. Believe what His Word says about you, not what the devil says about you.

Satan wants to bring you down—literally! God wants to lift you up!

"For I know the plans that I have for you," **declares the Lord,** **"plans for welfare and not for calamity to give you a future and a hope."** **(Jeremiah 29:11)**

His promise to Israel is His promise to us.

And if you belong to Christ, then you are Abraham's descendants [seed], heirs according to promise. **(Galatians 3:29)**

We have the promises of God, but we also have the responsibility to be effectual in and through our obedience to God.

Is it not sad that the forgiveness our Father gives so freely when we ask, we hold on to so tightly when others ask?

When you are troubled or distressed, do you go to the source, the only One who could meet your need?

Have you ever encouraged (strengthened) yourself in the Lord with His Word, taking His promises for yourself?

Do you see yourself as Abraham's seed, receiving the same promises?

Jonah's Dilemma

～

I am reminded of Jonah and how he chose to hold on to unforgiveness concerning the people of Nineveh.

Jonah 1-4 tells how God called Jonah to go to Nineveh and proclaim in the streets that their wickedness was seen by God and that He was giving them a chance to repent. Jonah did not want to do what God had asked him to, so he ran away. Now Jonah had a reason for not wanting the Ninevites to be forgiven, or so he thought.

The Ninevites were a fierce people, and Jonah could not forget who they were or forgive what they had done to Israel. There was no way he wanted God to forgive them, so he tried to run instead of being obedient. Imagine thinking he could hide from God!

After a series of circumstances that brought Jonah back to the realization that he could neither run nor hide from God, and after reconciling himself to what he was told to do, he proceeded to go to Nineveh. After he walked through the great city, preaching repentance, the people repented. This angered Jonah. He thought to himself, "How can a people so undeserving of forgiveness so easily receive forgiveness, and all they had to do was repent?"

The people of Nineveh had a choice. They could continue in their way and be annihilated, or repent and be saved. There is true repentance and feigned repentance. The people of Nineveh, realizing the mercy of God, truly repented, and God did not bring calamity on them.

Jonah would rather have died than to see his enemies be forgiven. *Unforgiveness* was what they deserved, and *unforgiveness* was what they should have received. A short time later, Jonah learned firsthand about God's mercy and compassion.

Do you relate to Jonah or to God? Jonah wanted to hold on to unforgiveness. God holds out forgiveness to anyone who asks in repentance.

Have you ever run or wanted to run from God when He asked you to do something?

Have you ever held a different attitude when He asked you to forgive someone, because you believed he or she went too far or did too much against God or you to be worthy to receive forgiveness, no matter how much they sought it?

Have you looked back on your life and found that you also

were a sinner and did much against God? Did you feel worthy to be forgiven?

IF YOU DO NOT FORGIVE, YOU WILL NOT BE FORGIVEN

And forgive us our debts, as we also have forgiven our debtors. (Matthew 6:12)

"For if you forgive others for their transgressions, your heavenly Father will also forgive you. "But if you do not forgive others, then your Father will not forgive your transgressions." (Matthew 6:14—15)

"And whenever you stand praying, forgive, if you have anything against anyone; so that your Father also who is in heaven may forgive you your transgressions. "But if you do not forgive, neither will your Father who is in heaven forgive your transgressions." (Mark 11:25—26)

In their simplicity, these Scriptures say that God will treat us as we treat others. It does not mean the forgiveness we received at our salvation is invalid; we have already been judged forgiven!

I believe these Scriptures are about a relational situation; a wedge we put between us and God because of disobedience and therefore, our relationship, our communion with Him suffers. We lose a part of our intimacy with God!

When we learn God's truth about the importance of not only being forgiven but of forgiving and choose not to, our relationship is hindered by purposely holding on to the sin of unforgiveness, but it will be gloriously restored when we repent and choose to obey God's command.

MEMORIES

M emories of the past that flood your mind might bring you to ... the nights that you thought you were safe until you heard the door-knob turn and an uninvited "guest" entered and changed your life ... or the beatings that you took, all the while wondering why it was happening ... or being told that you were not worth much ... or feeling that you could not or would not ever measure up. You can fill in the blanks. Do you really want to live your life that way?

The person or people who made you feel that your life as you knew it would never be the same may be the same people who experienced physical or mental torture themselves. It has been said that those who grow up in a drug, sexual, alcoholic, or abusive environment can tend to do the same to others.

Your life will change again for the better if you forgive whoever may have interrupted the life God intended for you. I am not saying that this kind of abuse is right—it is not. But if you want to live your life for God and for those you love, you must make the decision, or else you will be in bondage, in a type of prison.

To live the life that God has for you, you must use the key of forgiveness to open the prison door. There is *freedom* in forgiveness.

So if the Son makes you free, you will be free indeed. (John 8:36)

What was your childhood like?

Do you look back with joy or sadness?

Have you carried some of the baggage from your past into your present?

Is it hard to let go of your feelings from the past?

Have you taken to yourself the words spoken to you, the actions against you, the feelings of inadequacy and worthlessness?

Have you believed the lies, acting on them and becoming what they say you are, like a self-fulfilling prophecy?

Better yet, do you believe what God says you are in His eyes and leave all that is not of Him behind?

GOD'S LOVING DISCIPLINE

I n closing, I would like to share this experience with you: Soon after I became a child of
God, my precious little daughter had been doing
some things that she was not supposed to. She
would repeatedly come to me and say she was
sorry and ask for forgiveness. One time after she
asked, I responded in anger and said, "If you
were really sorry, you would not keep doing it!"

Even before the words came out of my mouth,
I was convicted and felt grieved in my spirit as
the Holy Spirit reminded me that I had repeatedly committed sins also and had continually
asked for forgiveness, and He had forgiven me.
He wanted me to put myself in her place and feel
as she did.

Oh, how God loves us—so much so that He
does not want us to stay as He found us, and I
felt that overwhelming love through His discipline.
God does not want us to continually commit the
same sins, but He wants us to remember how
He forgave and forgives. He does not want us
to take our freedom in Him lightly, but rather, to

have the desire to do as He does, acting and reacting as He does.

Have you experienced His loving discipline?
What have you learned through His discipline?
Does His discipline make you feel guilty, or does it make you feel loved?
Do you think He would do anything that was not out of love?
My greatest desire is to walk with my God as He desires me to!

Before we arrive at our destination, I have two Scriptures that I would love to share with you. They speak volumes to me, and I pray they will to you also:

He must increase, but I must decrease. (John 3:30)

What I believe John was saying is that the only way Jesus can be in control is for us (self, ego) to relinquish control, to become as nothing in comparison, to allow Him to be strong in our weaknesses. It is no longer about us when we become His!

I have been crucified with Christ; and it is no longer I who live, but Christ lives in me; and the life which I now live in the flesh I live by faith in the Son of God, who loved me and gave Himself up for me. (Galatians 2:20)

Did you hear that in your spirit? By becoming His, my identity and your identity are no longer in self, but gloriously, joyfully beyond words, our identity is in Christ!

I pray that the journey we have taken together has helped bring you to this place of forgiveness. What a beautiful place it is! We can take some time here and enjoy all that Father has for us. Do not worry about the time; He will see you home.

I enjoyed our time together. I hope you did too.
To God be all glory, honor, and praise!

Conclusion

~~~

Belonging to God is the greatest joy, but it is also a great responsibility. We are representing He who made heaven and earth, the Alpha and the Omega, the beginning and the end. Christ Jesus who loves us beyond what we can even imagine took our death sentence upon Himself, which is eternal separation from God because of sin. He defeated death so we could have eternal life with Him.

Whatever happens between you and another, remember that it is better to ask God to change what needs to be changed in you than to ask God to change the other. Obedience to Him is what brings the blessing.

Do not be too quick to talk to others about your circumstance, but, may I say, be quick to talk to God about it and to follow His leading. He will always lead you in the right way—His way!

Oh, how I thank God for His love, mercy, compassion, and forgiveness for me and all who come to Him with a repentant heart! How thankful I am to Him that He loves me so much that He cares about my actions in thought, word, and deed, desiring to teach me what pleases Him. I am grateful for every time He brings to my attention something that draws me closer to Him. I am never saddened, but rather, joyful for His counsel and for His direction. I ask Him to change what needs to be changed in me so that I will be the daughter He wants me to be. I so much desire to be like Him!

I have seen a phrase that says, *"The greatest gift you will ever give the world is your intimacy with God."* How true those words are!

CPSIA information can be obtained at www.ICGtesting.com
Printed in the USA
LVOW12s2042270515

440145LV00014B/95/P